MONROE COUNTY LIBRARY SYSTEM
MONROE MICHIGAN 48161

D1412183

CULTURE IN ACTION

Neil Gaiman

ROCK STAR WRITER

Charlotte Guillain

Chicago, Illinois

www.heinemannraintree.com
Visit our website to find out more information about Heinemann-Raintree books.

To order:

☎ Phone 888-454-2279

🖳 Visit www.heinemannraintree.com to browse our catalog and order online.

© 2011 Raintree
an imprint of Capstone Global Library, LLC
Chicago, Illinois

Visit our website at www.heinemannraintree.com

All rights reserved. No part of this publication may be reproduced or transmitted in any form or by any means, electronic or mechanical, including photocopying, recording, taping, or any information storage and retrieval system, without permission in writing from the publisher.

Edited by Louise Galpine and Diyan Leake
Designed by Victoria Allen
Original illustrations © Capstone Global Library Ltd 2011
Illustrated by Randy Schirz
Picture research by Hannah Taylor

Originated by Capstone Global Library Ltd
Printed in and bound in China by CTPS

14 13 12 11 10
10 9 8 7 6 5 4 3 2 1

Library of Congress Cataloging-in-Publication Data
Guillain, Charlotte.
  Neil Gaiman : rock star writer / Charlotte Guillain.
    p. cm. -- (Culture in action)
  Includes bibliographical references and index.
  ISBN 978-1-4109-3929-6
  1. Gaiman, Neil--Juvenile literature. 2. Authors, English--20th century--Biography--Juvenile literature. I. Title.
  PR6057.A319Z67 2011
  823'.914--dc22
  [B]
                            2009052815

Acknowledgments
The author and publishers are grateful to the following for permission to reproduce copyright material: Alamy Images pp. **13** (© Mark Phillips), **16** (© Photos 12), **18** (© Radius Images), **24** (© Photos 12); American Library Association p. **19**; Corbis pp. **5** (Reuters/Richard Clement), **22** (Bettmann); Getty Images pp. **4** (WireImage/Mark Sullivan), **10** (Bloomberg/Daniel Acker), **20** (Redferns/Marc Broussely), **25** (FilmMagic/Jeff Kravitz); Image supplied by the Marion E. Wade Center, Wheaton College, Wheaton, IL p. **7**; The Kobal Collection p. **14** (Paramount); Lebrecht Music & Arts p. **17** (Drew Farrel); Mary Evans Picture Library p. **6** (The Francis Frith Collection); Photolibrary p. **8** (Creatas); Rex Features pp. **9** (Gunter W. Kienitz), **12** (Richard Saker), **23** (© Paramount/Everett); shutterstock pp. **26** (© design56), **27** (© Cora Reed).

Cover photograph of Neil Gaiman reproduced with permission of Corbis (Retna/Seth Kushner).

We would like to thank Saimma Dyer, Scot Smith, and Jackie Murphy for their invaluable help in the preparation of this book.

Every effort has been made to contact copyright holders of any material reproduced in this book. Any omissions will be rectified in subsequent printings if notice is given to the publisher.

Disclaimer
All the Internet addresses (URLs) given in this book were valid at the time of going to press. However, due to the dynamic nature of the Internet, some addresses may have changed, or sites may have changed or ceased to exist since publication. While the author and publisher regret any inconvenience this may cause readers, no responsibility for any such changes can be accepted by either the author or the publisher.

Author
Charlotte Guillain is an experienced children's author and editor. Her favorite Neil Gaiman book is *The Day I Swapped My Dad for Two Goldfish*.

Literacy consultant
Jackie Murphy is Director of Arts at the Center of Teaching and Learning, Northeastern Illinois University. She works with teachers, artists, and school leaders internationally.

Contents

Some words are printed in bold, **like this**. You can find out what they mean by looking in the glossary on page 30.

Who Is Neil Gaiman?

What do you know about Neil Gaiman? Perhaps you have seen his picture books or read some of his award-winning **novels**, such as *The Graveyard Book*. Maybe you are a **comic book** fan and have discovered *The Books of Magic*. Or have you enjoyed the movie version of his book *Coraline*?

Neil is a writer who cannot be summed up in just one sentence. He is happy writing for adults and children, for the screen, and for a single reader. He works well with illustrators, other writers, and filmmakers. His many fans follow the **blog** he posts on the Internet in the same way other fans follow rock stars. In fact, before he started writing books, Neil wrote about popular recording artists.

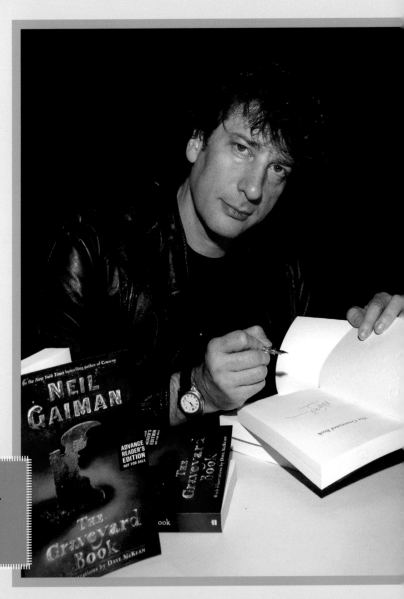

Neil's stories are a mix of the mystery and darkness in other worlds and of normal life in our ordinary world.

Neil has many fans who enjoy hearing him speak at book festivals and award ceremonies.

New worlds

Neil Gaiman's writing is often described as **fantasy**. This is a type of writing that explores the idea of magic and the **supernatural**. Many of Neil's stories describe another world alongside the real world we know. People and creatures can move between these different worlds, leading to strange and amazing events.

Fantasy writers

Some other authors who are writing for children and teens include Lemony Snicket, J. K. Rowling, Angie Sage, Rick Riordan, Stephenie Meyer, Philip Pullman, and Chris Riddell. Have you read any others? Neil's favorite fantasy book for children is *Archer's Goon* by Diana Wynne Jones. He says she is "the best writer of magical children's fiction of our generation."

Growing Up

Neil Gaiman was born on November 10, 1960. His family was **Jewish** and originally came from Poland before settling near the south coast of England. His father joined the army and then worked in the family chain of grocery stores. He hated this job, so after he married Neil's mother, a pharmacist, they moved to an English town called East Grinstead and opened a health food store. Neil grew up in this small town with his two younger sisters.

This is how East Grinstead looked when Neil was a young boy there.

Books

Neil always loved reading and carried a book with him wherever he went. He enjoyed reading books by C. S. Lewis, J. R. R. Tolkien, E. Nesbit, Edgar Allen Poe, and Michael Moorcock. He also loved ancient legends and myths (ancient stories).

Narnia

One of Neil's favorite childhood books was the *Voyage of the Dawn Treader*. This was one of C. S. Lewis's seven Narnia stories. Lewis took ideas from ancient Greek myths as well as medieval Irish legends and created his own magical world of Narnia. In *The Lion, the Witch and the Wardrobe*, characters travel to Narnia through a wardrobe. Neil uses a similar idea in *Coraline*, where the characters move between worlds through a bricked-in door.

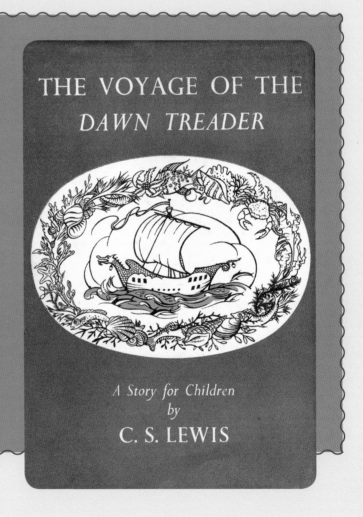

THE VOYAGE OF THE DAWN TREADER

A Story for Children by

C. S. LEWIS

Mythology

When Neil was 12 years old, he spent time with his Jewish cousins and began studying for his **bar mitzvah**. His teacher, Reb Meyer Lev, was very interested in the stories from Jewish **mythology**, and he was happy to share these with Neil. Neil has used ideas from many of these ancient myths in his own writing. Neil says, "I love mythology. Mythology excites me [to] no end."

When Jewish boys are 13 years old, they celebrate their bar mitzvah. This means they are old enough to be responsible for their own religious observance.

Science fiction

As a teenager, Neil became interested in the **genre** of writing called **science fiction**. It is similar to **fantasy**, but explores ideas that could be scientifically possible. Science fiction is often set in the future or in outer space.

Becoming a writer

When Neil was in school, he told a guidance counselor that he wanted to write **comic books** for a living. He was advised to become an accountant, but instead started working as a journalist. He wrote for many magazines and wrote articles about the fantasy books he loved so much. Neil enjoyed interviewing people and writing articles. However, he did not like the way newspapers **edited** what he had written.

Band biography

Neil's first published book was a **biography** of the 1980s pop band Duran Duran. This English band was part of the New Romantic music scene. This was a time when many musicians wore incredible makeup, had big hairstyles, and wore unusual clothes. Duran Duran reunited in 2000 and still plays today.

Comics

Through his work as a journalist, Neil met Alan Moore, a **comic book** writer who encouraged him to write for comics. Neil's first comic strips were published in the comic *2000 AD*. Neil was then asked to write the Miracle Man comic book stories. Miracle Man was a superhero that had first been created in the 1960s.

Sandman and beyond

In 1989 Neil created his version of the comic book character Sandman. The Sandman series was published for adults. It was very successful and won many awards. It was about a character named Morpheus, the Lord of Dreams, who has been imprisoned by wizards. Neil also wrote *The Books of Magic*, which were about a boy who learns he could be a great wizard.

Away from work, things were also going well. Neil got married in the mid-1980s and soon had a son, Michael, and a daughter, Holly.

Neil Gaiman's success as a writer of comic books has gained him a wide audience of readers.

Create a comic book hero

Try creating and drawing your own comic book hero, like Miracle Man and Sandman.

Steps to follow:

1. Think of all the superheroes you know, such as Spiderman and Batman. Heroes have special powers that they use to fight villains and protect the public. They each have a unique costume that tells us about who they are. All have a weakness—for example, green kryptonite takes away Superman's power. All have a secret identity—for example, Spiderman is really Peter Parker.

2. Choose a name for your superhero—it could be a man or a woman. Do you want your hero to be connected to an animal? If so, what makes that animal special? Does it live underwater? Does it move quickly? Do you want your hero to have a name that reflects where she lives or what he does, such as Shadowgirl or Mindreader Man?

3. Choose two or three special powers for your hero. Then think of a weakness. Decide what your hero's costume and secret identity could be.

4. Now draw your superhero in his or her costume on a large piece of paper. Use paints, felt, and glitter. Label your picture to show your hero's special powers and weaknesses.

Moving into Other Formats

Neil has said, "Given the choice between doing something successful I've already done, and doing something I've never done before and risking making a complete idiot of myself, I will do the something I've never done before." During the 1990s, he tried writing in many different **formats**.

In 1990 Neil began writing a **novel** for adults, *Good Omens*, with the writer Terry Pratchett. Unlike many writers, Neil is used to working very closely with **comic book** illustrators, and maybe this is why he was able to work so well with another writer.

Sir Terry Pratchett

Like Neil, Terry was a journalist before becoming a very popular **fantasy novelist**. His many novels include the Discworld series of books. His children's novel, *The Amazing Maurice and His Educated Rodents*, won the Carnegie Medal in 2001. *Nation*, another novel, has also received many awards.

The traditional English Punch and Judy puppet show was the inspiration for Neil's graphic novel.

New directions

Neil's second daughter, Maddy, was born in 1994. In the same year Neil's **graphic novel**, *The Tragical Comedy or Comical Tragedy of Mr. Punch*, was published. Graphic novels use pictures and words like comic books, but they tell a complete story. Comic books tell part of an ongoing story so readers have to buy each part of a serial. Neil thinks *Mr. Punch* is one of the best things he has written.

In 1996 *Neverwhere*, Neil's television series, was made in the United Kingdom. This series explored "London Below," a strange and frightening world underneath the real city of London, England. Neil published an adult novel of this story at the same time.

Novels

Neil started to become as well-known as a novelist as he was for his comic books and graphic novels. His novel *Stardust* was published in 1998. The artist Charles Vess provided pictures for an illustrated version of this dark and comical fairy story and won an award for these illustrations. Neil and Charles had already worked together on many comic books.

After this, Neil returned to focus on Sandman, first with an illustrated novel called *The Dream Hunters* and then a graphic novel in 2003, called *Endless Nights*. He also managed to find time to write a novel for adults, *American Gods*, which was published in 2001. It became a New York Times best-seller and won the Nebula and Hugo Awards for best fantasy novel.

The illustrations of Charles Vess were brought to life in a movie version of *Stardust* (2007).

From prose to script

In a group or pair, try acting out a part from one of Neil's books. Find these books in the library and read these or other sections you would like to try performing. Some scenes you might like to try are:

- From *Coraline*, when Coraline meets her "other" parents for the first time
- From *The Wolves in the Walls*, when Lucy and her family run out of the house and Lucy then goes back for her pig
- In a larger group you could act out *The Day I Swapped My Dad for Two Goldfish*

Steps to follow:

1. Choose who will act each character's part. Decide if you need to make up any extra conversations to tell the audience important details. Do you need a **narrator** to tell the audience what is happening?

2. Decide if you need any **props**. These are objects that are part of the story (for example, Lucy's pig or a goldfish bowl).

3. Think about how your character is feeling in the scene and how you can show this. Use your voice, face, and movements to try out different ideas.

4. Perform the scene for another group.

Children's Books

During the 1990s, Neil's three children were growing up. Being a father affected his ideas and interests. He started writing his first children's **novel**, *Coraline*, for his daughter Holly. It took him 11 years to write the story, and during that time he moved to the United States. By the time he finished the book, he had his youngest daughter, Maddy, in mind. The book was published in 2002.

Coraline

As a child, Neil loved to explore gardens and lived in a house with a bricked-in door, just like his character Coraline. In the book she finds another world behind this door, where a sinister "other" family lives. Coraline has to bravely face her fears and rescue her parents from her fake mother, who has buttons for eyes. Neil wanted to write about a feisty "heroine who doesn't get saved by boys."

The Wolves in the Walls has been performed on stage as a **musical**.

Picture stories

Coraline was followed in 2003 by two picture books for younger readers. One was *The Day I Swapped My Dad for Two Goldfish*, which was originally published in 1997. The other one was *The Wolves in the Walls*. These books were illustrated by the artist Dave McKean, who had worked with Neil for many years. In *The Wolves in the Walls* another heroine, Lucy, has to bravely confront nightmarish wolves and get her home back.

Inspiration

Neil watched his children play and fight together. He may have used some of these memories when he wrote *The Day I Swapped My Dad for Two Goldfish*. In this story the older brother is mean to his younger sister and she enjoys watching him getting into trouble. Despite this, they stick together throughout the story.

Neil has often chosen graveyards and other scary places as the setting for his stories.

Magical books

Neil's next book, *M is for Magic*, was a collection of short stories with a dark and sinister edge. One of these stories, "The Witch's Headstone," describes a boy who is raised in a graveyard. Neil was to return to this idea later. In 2007 Neil also published a novel for young people, *Interworld*.

On stage

In 2008 the Rogue Artists Ensemble in Los Angeles, California, performed *The Tragical Comedy or Comical Tragedy of Mr. Punch* on stage. The story describes a boy's adventures when he visits his grandfather's seaside arcade. The theater company used Dave McKean's illustrations from the **graphic novel** as well as puppets, masks, and dancing.

Medal winner

Neil published two books in 2008, *Odd and the Frost Giants* and *The Graveyard Book*. *The Graveyard Book* won the Newbery Medal in 2009. The book explores further Neil's idea of a boy being raised by the dead people in a graveyard. The boy, Bod, escaped from the murderer who killed his family and is now protected and helped by ghosts as he grows up. He is finally able to survive in the two worlds of the living and the dead.

Newbery Medal

The Newbery Medal is an award given to children's writers in the United States. It was the first award in the world given for children's literature and has been won by authors such as Louis Sachar for *Holes* and Katherine Paterson for *Bridge to Terabithia*. Neil was "thrilled and honored" to win the Newbery Medal and said, "I think children's literature is the most important that there is."

Poems and pictures

Several of Neil's picture books for children are illustrated poems. *The Dangerous Alphabet* tells the story in verse of two treasure-seeking children who face the dangers of monsters and pirates. Like traditional alphabet books, it includes the words "A is for …, B is for …" but Neil plays with this structure. The book has funny, detailed illustrations by Gris Grimly. *Crazy Hair* is a nonsense poem describing the many wonderful creatures living in the **narrator's** hair. The amazing pictures are by Dave McKean.

Poetic present

Blueberry Girl was originally a poem written for Neil's friend, the singer Tori Amos. She was expecting a baby daughter and Neil wrote the poem as a gift to her. He read the poem at several events, and people began to ask about it. He decided to publish it as a book. It was illustrated by Charles Vess.

The friendship between Tori Amos and Neil Gaiman has influenced her work as a singer as well as his as a writer.

Writing a poem

The Dangerous Alphabet is a 26-line poem that describes a dangerous adventure. Borrow a copy from the library and look at how the alphabet is built into the poem. Each line refers to a letter of the alphabet and includes a word that begins with this letter—for example, "A is for Always, that's where we embark; B is for Boat pushing off in the dark ..."

Why don't you try writing an alphabet poem?

Steps to follow:

1. Choose a title for your poem with a different adjective than "dangerous"—for example, *The Magical Alphabet*, *The Funny Alphabet*, or *The Mysterious Alphabet*.

2. Try writing a poem that describes magical, funny, or mysterious things or events using the alphabet as your structure. Experiment with the letters of the alphabet and brainstorm the different words you could use.

3. Don't be afraid to cheat! Neil uses the letter "C" to mean "see" in his poem! Have fun bending the rules.

4. If you illustrate your poem, you can tell more of the story using pictures.

5. Share your poem by reading it aloud to your friends.

A is for...

21

Making Movies

Many of Neil's stories have been adapted for the screen. *MirrorMask* was released in 2005 and was directed by Neil's old friend and working partner, Dave McKean. The movie tells the story of a young girl, Helena, who fights with her mother and wants to run away. But her mother becomes sick, and Helena actually finds herself in another world of dark shadows. She has to fight to find her way home to be reunited with her parents. These are similar ideas to those explored in *Coraline*.

Jim Henson

Neil and Dave worked with the Jim Henson Company to make the movie *MirrorMask*. Jim Henson was a U.S. puppeteer who worked on the television shows *Sesame Street* and *The Muppets*. He also created amazing puppets for movies, such as Yoda in the *Star Wars* films. Jim Henson died in 1990, but the Jim Henson Company still makes puppets for movies and television shows.

Stardust

A movie version of Neil's fairy story *Stardust* was made in 2007. Many changes were made to the original story, and sections were left out so that the movie would not be too long. But it has the same central story, about a young man who goes to a magical land to find a fallen star for the girl he loves. Neil helped the scriptwriters write the **screenplay** and was involved in choosing the actors. The movie's designers tried to keep the look and feel of Charles Vess's original illustrations. Both Neil and Charles were happy with the movie.

Many famous actors starred in the movie *Stardust*, including Robert De Niro and Michelle Pfeiffer.

Animation

Neil has also been involved with **animated** movies. One of the best-known is *Coraline*, made by the **animator** Henry Selick. A new character, a boy named Wybie, was introduced in the movie as someone for Coraline to share her thoughts with. He owns the black cat that helps her in the **novel**. Neil loves the movie and calls it "Coraline as seen through Henry's world." Even he finds it scary!

Neil had seen animated movies such as *James and the Giant Peach* and *The Nightmare Before Christmas* by Henry Selick and was impressed by his work. This photo shows Henry working on the set of *Coraline*.

This photo shows the cast and other people who worked on the movie of *Coraline*, including Dakota Fanning (wearing pink), who provided Coraline's voice.

Silent film

In 2009 Neil directed a short silent film for adults called *Statuesque* that was shown on British television on Christmas Day. One of the stars was his girlfriend, the singer Amanda Palmer. It is a story about a man who is in love with a woman who performs in the street as a living statue. Liam McKean, the son of the illustrator Dave McKean, also acted in the movie. He played a hip-hop dancing statue. The people playing the statues nearly froze standing still in the cold as Neil filmed them!

Stop-motion animation

Henry Selick makes animated movies using a technique called stop-motion. Another famous stop-motion animator is Nick Park, who makes the Wallace and Gromit movies. Stop-motion animation means puppets are gradually moved and filmed to show the action. Everything in Selick's films is hand-made, including puppets, **props**, and sets. Around 450 people helped to make the *Coraline* movie, including someone whose job was to knit all the tiny clothes for the puppets!

Neil Gaiman Today

Today, Neil Gaiman is as busy as ever. He is now divorced but still good friends with his ex-wife, who lives next door to his home near Minneapolis, Minnesota.

Writing habits

Neil has said that he sometimes stays up writing until 4:30 a.m., and so he often gets up around 10 a.m. He has a **gazebo** on the grounds of his house where he likes to write. Neil says, "When I'm writing a **novel**, I write in fountain pen, in a notebook. I often have two different pens and two colors of ink on the go [at any given time], to see at a glance how much I wrote in a day."

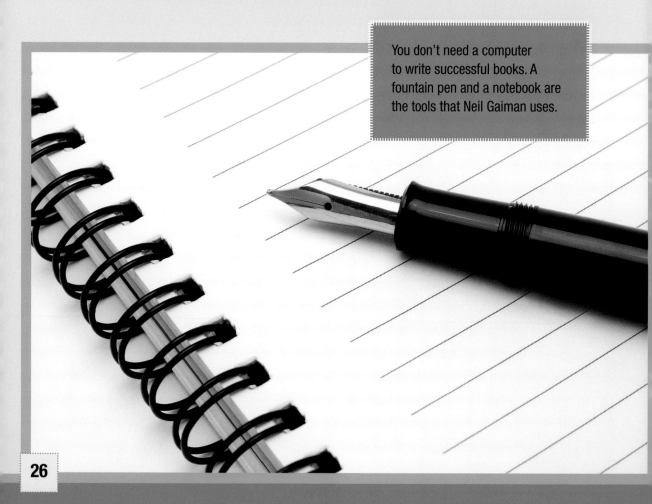

You don't need a computer to write successful books. A fountain pen and a notebook are the tools that Neil Gaiman uses.

What's next?

In 2009 Neil wrote a new Batman **comic book** story and he directed a silent film. He also worked with Charles Vess on a new illustrated poem, *Instructions*. It is impossible to guess what Neil will do next, but it will be something surprising and fantastical. Neil has written on his **blog** about how busy his life can be, but how important it is to look for the magic in the world around us. One night he stopped working to lie on his back and watch the stars: "I didn't mind that I couldn't think of anything to wish for … I could have stared up at the sky forever."

Neil about writing

- "I start off a story when I know where it begins; and the dialogue is something I mostly do by being quiet and listening."
- Advice for would-be writers: "Write. Finish things. Keep writing. And read everything."

Neil's many fans will line up to hear him read, or for book signings.

Timeline

1960	Neil is born in Portchester, near Portsmouth, on the south coast of England
1965	Neil's family moves to East Grinstead, in England
1977	Neil leaves school
1983	Neil's son, Michael, is born
1984	Neil's first short story is published
1985	Neil co-writes a book of quotations from **science fiction** called *Ghastly Beyond Belief*
	Neil's **biography** of the band Duran Duran is published
	Neil marries Mary McGrath
	Neil's daughter Holly is born
1986	Neil's first comic strips are published
1988	Neil's book *Don't Panic: The Official Hitchhiker's Guide to the Galaxy Companion* is published, about Douglas Adams and his books
1989	Neil starts to write the Sandman **comic books**
1990	*The Books of Magic* comic books are published
	Good Omens, a **novel** co-written with Terry Pratchett, is published
1991	Neil wins a World **Fantasy** Award for a Sandman story
1992	Neil moves to Minneapolis, Minnesota
1994	Neil's daughter Maddy is born

1994	The **graphic novel** *The Tragical Comedy or Comical Tragedy of Mr. Punch* is published
1996	The novel *Neverwhere* is published and a television version is shown in the United Kingdom
1998	The novel *Stardust* is published
2002	The novel *Coraline* is published
2003	The picture books *The Day I Swapped My Dad for Two Goldfish* and *The Wolves in the Walls* are published
2005	The movie *MirrorMask* is released
2007	The movie version of *Stardust* is released
	M is for Magic and *Interworld* are published
2008	The novels *The Graveyard Book* and *Odd and the Frost Giants* are published
	The picture book *The Dangerous Alphabet* is published
	Neil and Mary divorce
2009	The **animated** movie of *Coraline* is released
	The Graveyard Book wins the Newbery Medal
	The picture books *Crazy Hair* and *Blueberry Girl* are published
2010	Neil is made Honorary Chair of National Library Week in the United States
	The Graveyard Book wins the Carnegie Medal

Glossary

animated using moving models or illustrations

animator person who makes animated movies

bar mitzvah when Jewish boys are old enough to take responsibility for their own religious practice (at the age of 13)

biography life story

blog website where people comment or write diary entries

comic book magazine that tells a part of a longer serialized story, using words and illustrations

edit correct and adjust text before it is published

fantasy type of writing that explores the idea of magic and the supernatural

format way that a creative work is presented. Books are one format and movies are another.

gazebo small shed-like structure, usually with a view of the landscape

genre style or type of writing

graphic novel story that uses words and pictures like a comic but is bound like a book and tells a complete story

Jewish relating to Jews and their religion, Judaism

musical stage or movie performance of a story told with singing and dancing

mythology collection of myths (stories) belonging to a group of people, such as the ancient Greeks. The myths are usually about their history, gods, and heroes.

narrator person who recounts events in a story or performance

novel long fictional story

novelist person who writes novels

prop object used in a play or other performance

science fiction type of writing that explores fantastical worlds in a way that involves science and technology

screenplay script of a movie

supernatural not of the natural world (for example, ghosts)

Find Out More

Books

Here is a list of some of Neil Gaiman's books, and when they were published:

The Books of Magic (1993)

Coraline (2002)

The Day I Swapped My Dad for Two Goldfish (1997; illustrated version, 2003)

The Wolves in the Walls (2003)

Interworld (2007)

M Is for Magic (2007)

Odd and the Frost Giants (2008)

The Graveyard Book (2008)

Websites

www.mousecircus.com
This is the official Neil Gaiman website for young readers. Find out more about his books, watch videos about his work, and find out more about Neil and the illustrators he has worked with.

www.coraline.com
This is the website for Henry Selick's movie version of *Coraline*.

www.dccomics.com/dckids
Neil has written comic books for DC Comics, and this is their website. There is lots of information as well as comic books you can read online.

Index